CHRISTMAS
ORNAMENTS
COLORING BOOK

This book is printed on just one side of the paper
to avoid bleed through. If using markers it may be helpful
to place a piece of paper or cardstock behide the page.

To view samples of these illustrations colored by the author please visit
www.lovelyleisure.me

LOVELY LEISURE

ILLUSTRATIONS BY PAULA PARRISH

I0189918

Christmas Ornaments Coloring Book
© 2015 Paula Parrish

All rights reserved. No part of this book may be reproduced or
transmitted in any form or by any means, electronic or mechanical,
without prior written consent from the author.

www.lovely-leisure.com

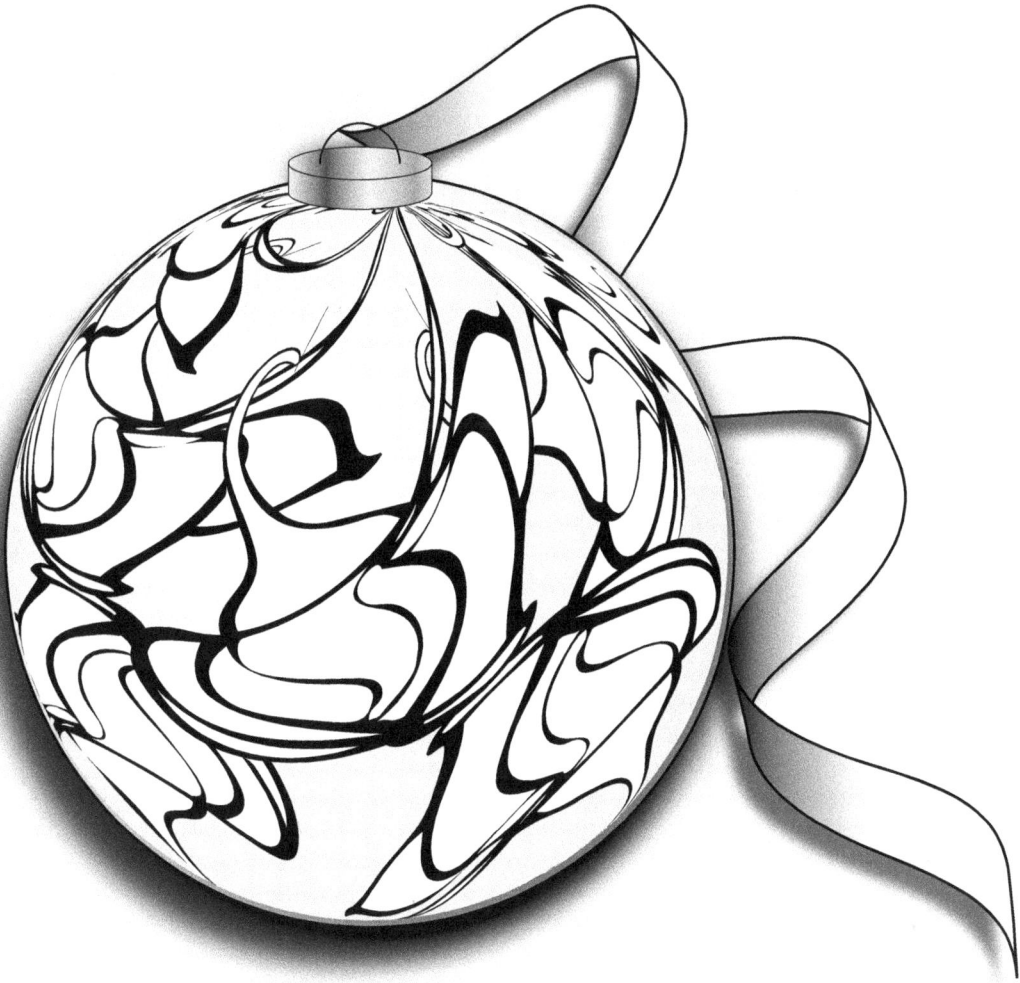

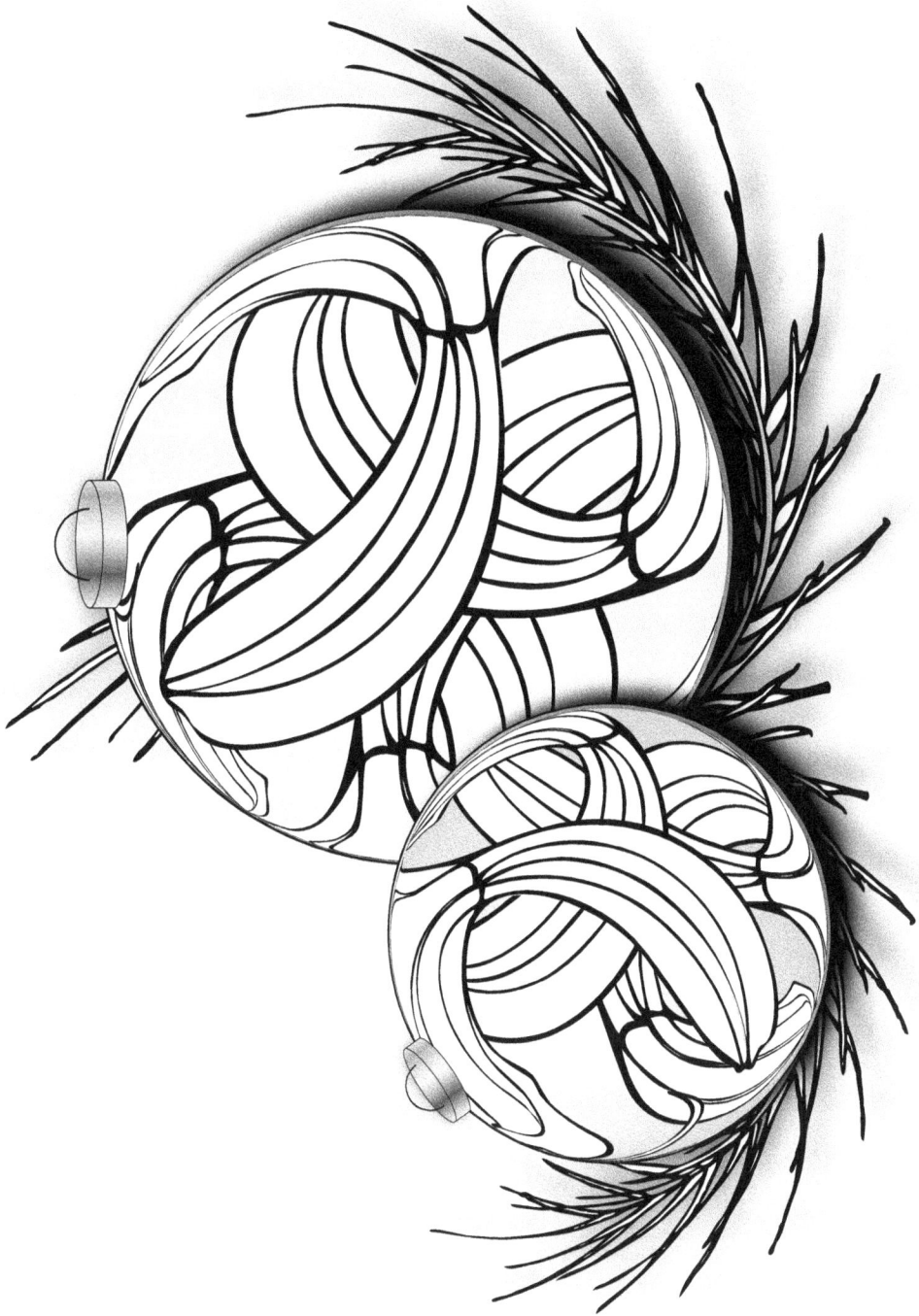

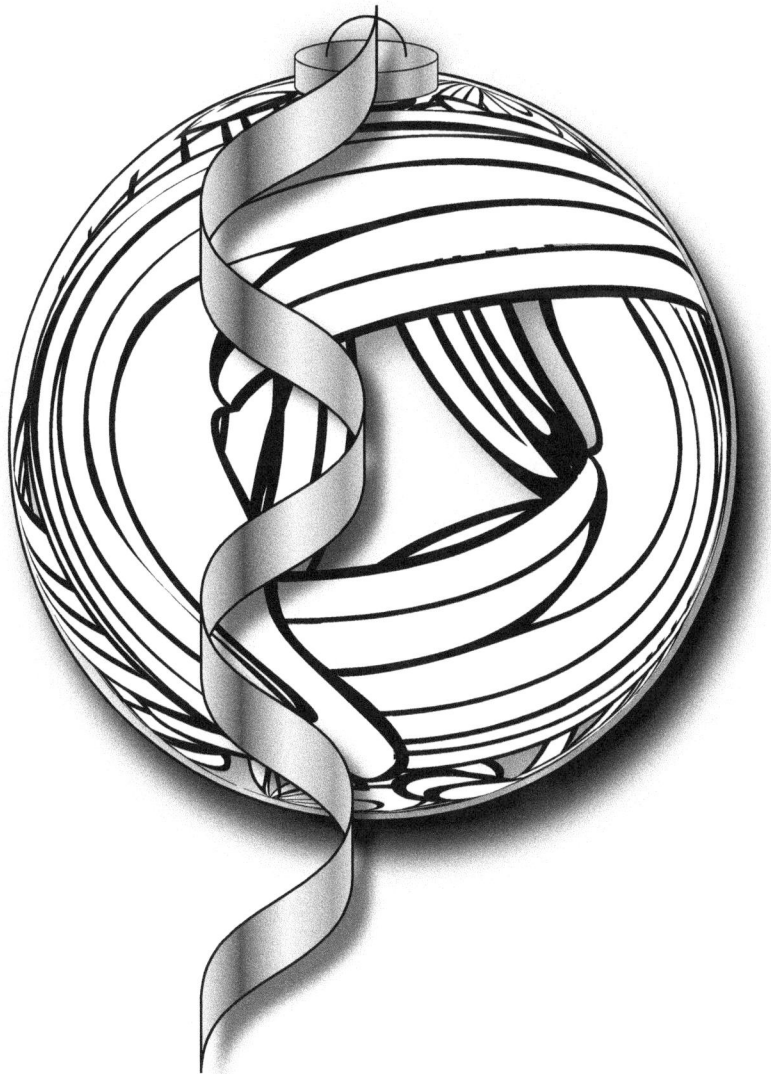

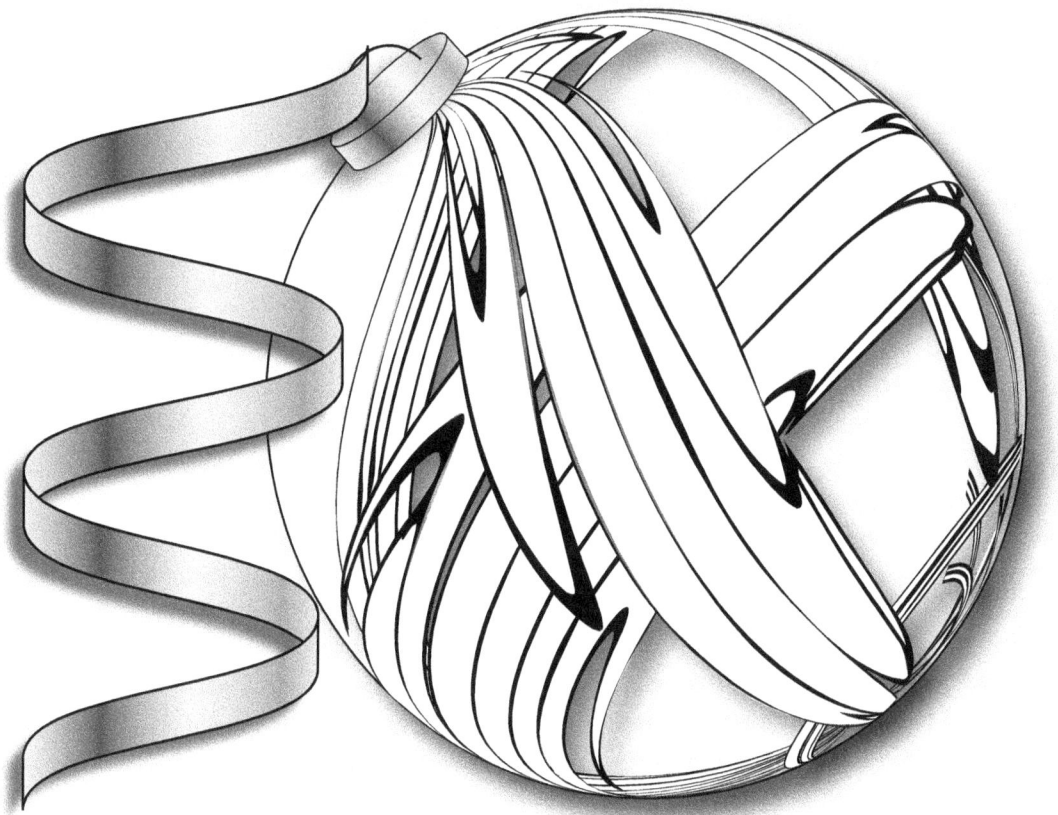

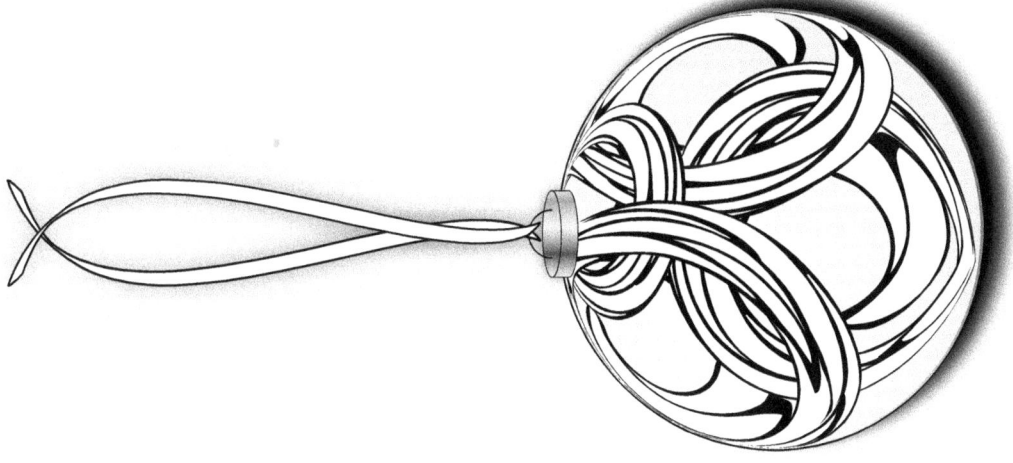
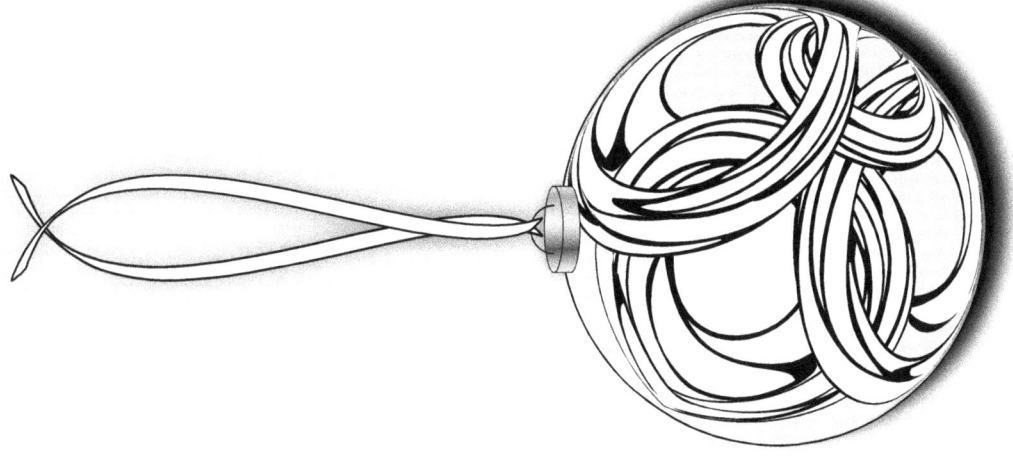

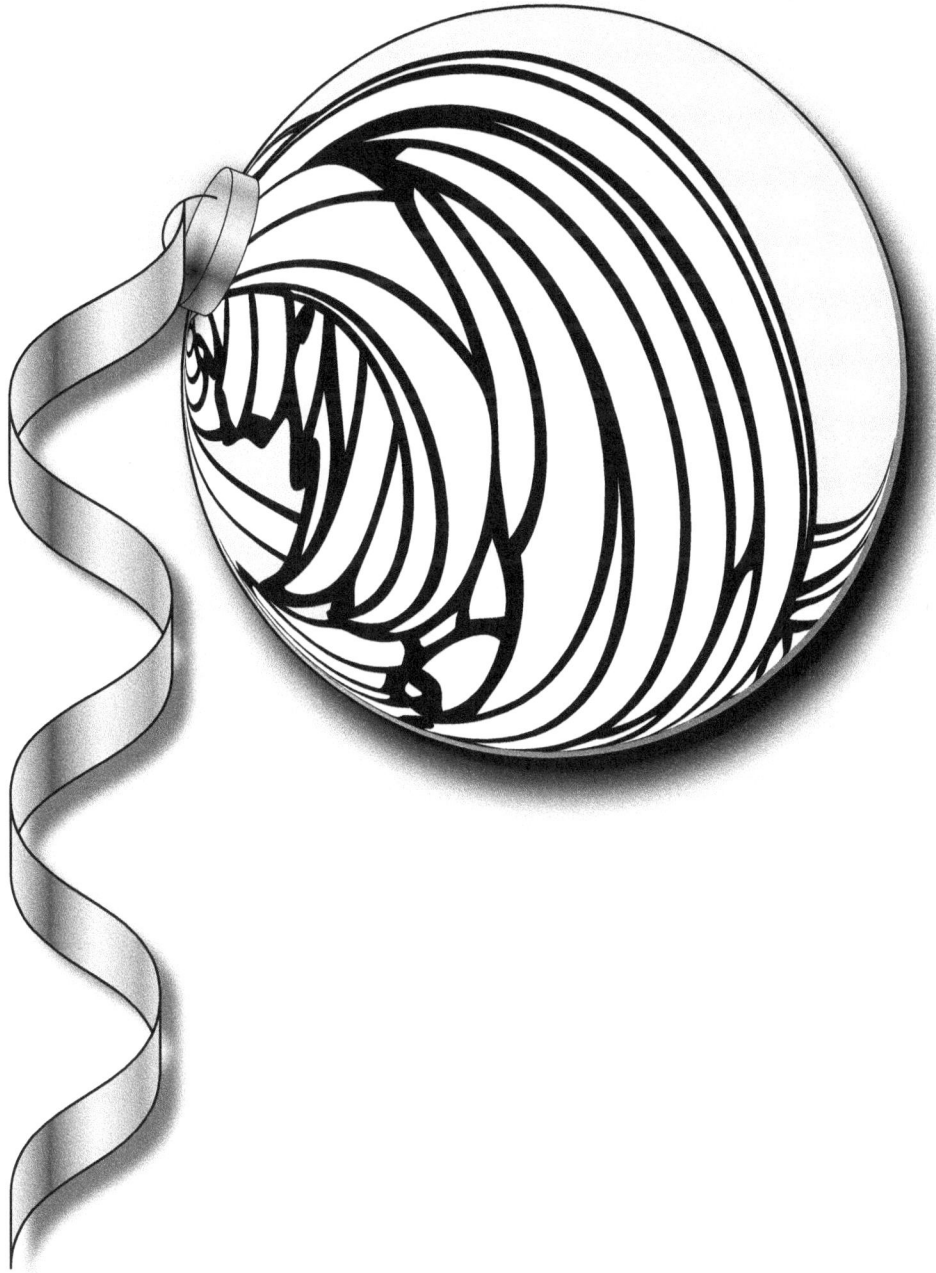

COLOR SWATCH TEST PAGE

Use this page to test and reference your colors

Christmas Ornaments Coloring Book
© 2015 Paula Parrish

To learn about current and upcoming books,
and view colored samples of the works contained herein,
please visit the author's website

www.lovely-leisure.com

I hope enjoy this book .
If are posting on facebook, the author appreciates if you would
please tag Paula Parrish or Lovely Leisure Coloring Books

www.ingramcontent.com/pod-product-compliance
Lightning Source LLC
Chambersburg PA
CBHW081226020426
42331CB00012B/3082